FACE READING ESSENTIALS

FOREHEAD, CHEEKS & CHIN

Face Reading Essentials - Forehead, Cheeks & Chin

Copyright © 2011 by Joey Yap
All rights reserved worldwide.
First Edition July 2011
Second Print December 2012

All intellectual property rights contained or in relation to this book belongs to Joey Yap.

No part of this book may be copied, used, subsumed, or exploited in fact, field of thought or general idea, by any other authors or persons, or be stored in a retrieval system, transmitted or reproduced in any way, including but not limited to digital copying and printing in any form whatsoever worldwide without the prior agreement and written permission of the author.

The author can be reached at:

Joey Yap Research International Sdn. Bhd. (939831- H)
19-3, The Boulevard, Mid Valley City,
59200 Kuala Lumpur, Malaysia.
Tel   : +603-2284 8080
Fax   : +603-2284 1218
Website : www.masteryacademy.com

DISCLAIMER:

The author, Joey Yap and the publisher, JY Productions Sdn Bhd, have made their best efforts to produce this high quality, informative and helpful book. They have verified the technical accuracy of the information and contents of this book. Any information pertaining to the events, occurrences, dates and other details relating to the person or persons, dead or alive, and to the companies have been verified to the best of their abilities based on information obtained or extracted from various websites, newspaper clippings and other public media. However, they make no representation or warranties of any kind with regard to the contents of this book and accept no liability of any kind for any losses or damages caused or alleged to be caused directly or indirectly from using the information contained herein.

Published by JY Productions Sdn. Bhd. (944330-D)

INDEX

The Forehead		15
1	High Forehead	16
2	Low Forehead	18
3	Smooth Forehead	20
4	Full or Fleshy Forehead	22
5	Beauty Beak	24
6	M Forehead	26
7	Square Forehead	28
8	Saw-Line Forehead	30
9	Receding Forehead	32
10	Protuding Forehead	34
11	Flat Forehead	36
12	Wide Forehead	38
13	Forehead with Narrow Bottom & Wider Top	40
14	Peaked Hairline	42
15	Rounded Hairline	44
16	Brow Ridge	46
17	No Brow Ridge	48
18	Self-Will Pad	50

額，顴，頦

The Cheeks		53
19	Large Cheeks	54
20	Small Cheeks	56
21	Wide Cheeks	58
22	Outward Growing Cheeks	60
23	Inward Growing Cheeks	62
24	Line Growing Across Cheeks	64
25	Stolen Spouse Mole	66
26	Healer Cheeks	68
27	High Cheekbones	70
28	Low Cheekbones	72
29	Thin Cheekbones	74
30	Orange peel cheeks	76
31	Pimple on cheeks	78
32	Mole on cheeks	80

The Chin		83
33	Large Chin	84
34	Small Chin	86
35	Long Chin	88
36	Double Chin	90
37	Protruding Chin	92
38	Receding Chin	94
39	Rounded Chin	96
40	Square Chin	98
41	Straight Chin	100
42	Cleft Chin	102
43	Jutting, Broad Chin	104
44	Pointed, Narrow Chin	106
45	Arch on Chin	108
46	Chin with Bumpy Appearance	110
47	Oval shape	112
48	Square shape	114
49	Scoop shape	116

額，顎，頦

The Essentials of Face Reading

The Face Reading Essentials series offers a crash course in the study of Mian Xiang (Chinese Art of Face Reading). Mian Xiang teaches us to 'read' the human face like a book. Face shape, structure, symmetry, face contours, features, facial expressions, Qi colours and more make up the overall picture when it comes to any given face. The raw data is there for anyone to see, Mian Xiang is simply a system which teaches anyone willing to learn to make sense of the story which each individual face tells.

There is a lot of information to process when you look at a face, and so I create the Face Reading Essentials series with the specific aim of breaking things down in a step by step manner for the layman.

The previous books in this series have been a resounding success with people keen to learn about Face Reading in a simple straightforward fashion. I have decided to expand upon the series with 5 new books, each of which is dedicated to a specific feature or aspect of Mian Xiang. My readers can now take their studies to the next level!

Mian Xiang instructs us to look either at specific points and features of the face (Fixed Position Reading 定流法) or, if we want to know more, to look at many features simultaneously and make sense of what they mean together (Combination Position Reading 混流法). Different features give us insight into different traits of the person in question. Combination Position Reading techniques give us a more in-depth analysis of a particular person but Fixed Position Reading represents an ideal starting point

for beginners. This technique is simple, easy to learn and effective, and accordingly, the Face Reading Essentials books deal with Fixed Position Reading.

The Forehead, Cheeks, and Chin

This book focuses on three particular areas of the face; the forehead, cheeks, and chin.

Your forehead is a one of the most important areas of the face, since it contains the Career, Life, Parents, Travelling, and Fortune and Virtue Palaces. In other words, the forehead represents your career and social status, as well as your intelligence. These things are intrinsically linked; for example, your intelligence may make or break your career and your career may in turn dictate your social status! When we learn about all three from an examination of someone's forehead we get a pretty good idea of where the person in question stands in life. The cheeks and cheekbones, known as the 'Power Bones', tell us about a person's willpower and ability to gain stature and wield authority.

Finally, the chin and jaws can give you clues about your later years in life (50+). These facial features also tell us about a person's affinity with their family and whether or not they can expect to enjoy wealth, support and help from family and children and have the peace of mind that goes with this support.

額，顙，頷

Face Reading and You

I've spent many years of my life researching various Face Reading methods and techniques, interpreting the classical texts of Mian Xiang and trying to extract the most important information for the modern age. The Face Reading Essentials books are meant to present this information to you in a relatively straightforward and easy-to-digest manner.

People aren't made to perfect specifications in a factory. Bear in mind that when you 'Face Read' someone, no one feature will perfectly match up to a 'type'. Sometimes people will possess several features which is why Face Reading requires you to do some insightful thinking of your own instead of trying to pigeon-hole everything mathematically. The answers you get from your Readings may not be black and white. The information presented here is categorized into types to that it may more easily be learned and understood but people don't always fall into types or categories. Face Reading is all about putting information together in creative ways, thinking about the context this information lies within and then piecing together a bigger picture. It is a good idea to study your own face in a mirror as you go along because practice really is the key to becoming an expert in Mian Xiang.

Should you wish to learn more about the intricacies of Mian Xiang study and practice, you might want to consider my *Homestudy Courses on Face Reading* (www.mianxianghomestudy.com). My earlier book, *Mian Xiang – Discover Face Reading* is a detailed, solid introduction to Mian Xiang, and my previous Face Reading Essentials series of books will also be helpful in your exploration.

Most importantly, be sure to enjoy Face Reading – because once you get a knack for 'Reading', you will find the practice pleasurable and enlightening. You will be surprised what you learn about yourself and others!

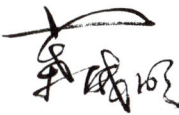

Joey Yap
July, 2011

Author's personal website	: www.joeyyap.com
Academy websites	: www.masteryacademy.com	www.baziprofiling.com
Joey Yap on Facebook	: www.facebook.com/joeyyapFB

The Three Regions of the Face

The face is divided into three significant regions, and these are the Forehead, Cheeks and Chin areas.

The Forehead refers to the area on the face that extends from above the eyebrow up towards the hairline of the temples. It is, in effect, the largest part of the face. The Forehead represents one's career and social status since both aspects of life are inextricably linked to one another. It denotes career prospects, intellect, capabilities, powers of observation and reasoning, nobility and credibility in life.

The Cheeks refer to the cheekbones, which are also known as Power Bones in Face Reading. It indicates a person's willpower as well as ability to wield power and represents his or her luck and fortunes in life, especially at ages 46 and 47.

The Chin forms part of the lower mandible or the lower jaw. It represents a person's life and fortunes in middle and old age.

額，顴，頦

Forehead

High Forehead 高额

How do you know if a forehead can be considered high? For men, it should be the width of five loosely-held fingers between the hairline and the eyebrows, while for women it should be four fingers.

The height of the forehead is a main indicator of intelligence. Therefore, a High Forehead denotes people with a relatively high level of intelligence or IQ. They have good analytical abilities, and great interpersonal and networking skills.

Such individuals have good career luck. When you see people with tall, broad and smooth scar-free foreheads, they are likely to be successful in their career. They also tend to come from a relatively happier childhood.

額，顛，頍

Low Forehead
低額

The Low Forehead is one that measures lesser than the five-finger (male) or four-finger (female) measurement between the hairline and the eyebrows.

As opposed to the High Forehead, the Low Forehead denotes a very hands-on person. People with this forehead prefer physical work or will do better working with their hands compared to tasks that require analytical thinking. They also dislike networking and socializing. There's a high probability that such person will also enter the workforce early in life.

Low Forehead individuals also have a hasty or temperamental character. Their impatience can likely get them into trouble. They may also come from a relatively unhappy childhood.

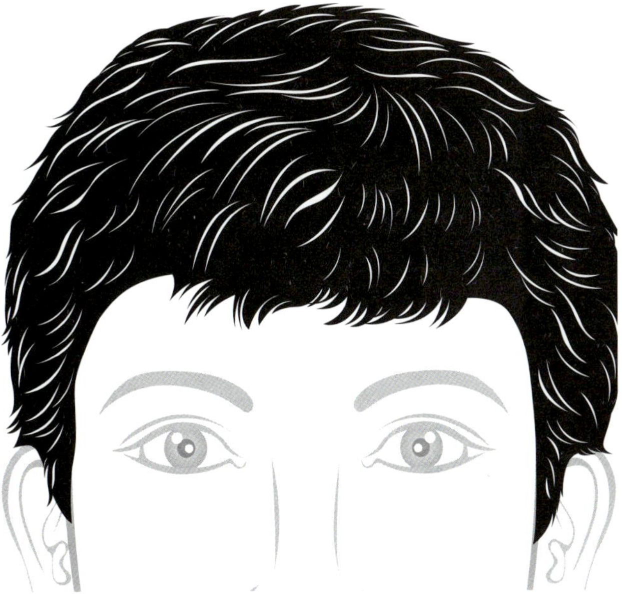

额,颡

Smooth Forehead
順滑額

The Smooth Forehead refers to a forehead without a trace of wrinkles, dents or scars. In short, it is clear and unblemished in any way.

People with Smooth Foreheads usually come from a good or at least above average family background, with loving and supportive parents. Thus, they tend to have a happy childhood.

With such background, they also have a better chance of pursuing higher or tertiary education and tend to have an abundance of good fortune before the age of thirty.

額，腦顴

Full or Fleshy Forehead
飽滿額

The Full or Fleshy Forehead refers to a forehead that has a substantial amount of flesh and possesses a full, plump appearance.

Individuals with foreheads that appear full or fleshy tend to encounter fewer or less severe obstacles in life. They also have the ability to flourish to thrive no matter how adverse circumstances may be. This is probably because this type of forehead signifies the presence of helpful people or Nobel Men in one's life. Individuals with this type of forehead will always have a helping hand at the right time, especially in times of need.

If the person has a Full and Rounded Forehead, he or she is likely to be creative and spontaneous in nature. People with such foreheads also prefer to approach things in their own terms and are most comfortable with solutions that works for them regardless of the acceptable norm.

額

Beauty Beak 美人喙

A Beauty Beak is where the hairline converges upon the middle of the forehead like a V. People with Beauty Beaks tend to be stubborn and rebellious.

Since the hairline also crosses the Parents Palace, men with Beauty Beaks are likely to not be able to see eye-to-eye with their father - although this rule is an exception if he is the only child. For women, this particular forehead indicates many unhappy romantic relationships with members of the opposite sex. They will probably end up marrying much older men.

It is not impossible for Beauty Beaked people to amass wealth by the time they reach 28. However, they should manage their fortune well as they are also likely to risk losing it by 30 and will have to start all over again.

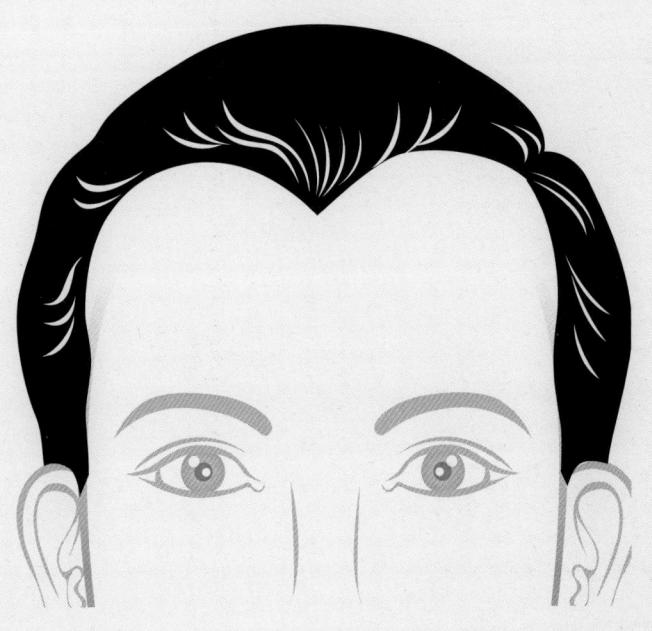

額，顙，頞

M Forehead M字形額

The M Forehead has an obvious hairline that looks like the letter 'M'.

People with such foreheads are creative and artistically-inclined. They enjoy the good things in life and have this capability to mingle with high society, where their talents are widely admired and held in high regard. They also hold a wide appeal amongst members of the opposite sex.

On the flip side, they are not good at managing what they earn and then to always living beyond their means.

額，顙，頟

Square Forehead
方形額

The Square Forehead refers to one that has a straight, horizontal hairline. It is normally associated with the Earth element, which represents reliability and also a practical personality.

People with a Square Forehead are also action-oriented as they believe that actions speak louder than words. They can be depended upon to see things through successfully. Career-wise, they tend to do well in the accounting and financial fields.

A woman with such forehead is usually more dominant than her husband in deciding household matters.

额、颡、颖

Saw-Line Forehead
鋸齒狀髮線

A Saw-Line Forehead refers to the hairline that grows unevenly and randomly. It looks like the jagged teeth of a saw – hence, its name.

As the Parents Palace is nearest to the hairline, people with the Saw-Line Foreheads have a poor affinity with their parents, especially the father. If there are twirls on either side of the hairline, it indicates the absence of at least one of the parents due to death or separation.

This particular forehead is not favorable for women as it denotes that she will have a poor relationship with her significant other. She should also choose a husband who is more matured or senior – traditionally, ten years older - than her to avoid an unhappy marriage.

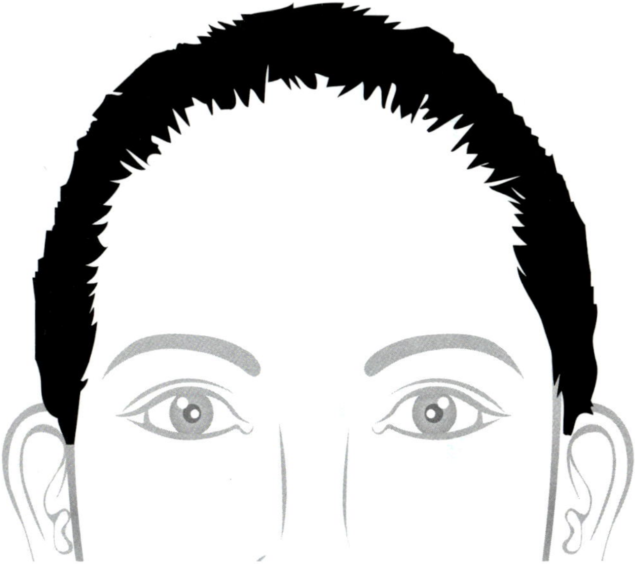

額,顙,

Receding Forehead
後縮額

A Receding Forehead is one that slants or angles backwards as viewed from the side profile.

This indicates a strong development of memory and quick mental reactions, which can also be perceived as a fast, albeit somewhat hasty, thinker. A person with this forehead tends to be impatient and is likely to act first without considering the consequences or be more thoughtful of his or her actions.

If the eyebrow bone is protruding at the end of the forehead's slop, it shows that this person also enjoys good luck on his or her side. However, such luck can also be superficial as this person may make his or her fortune by 28, and only to lose it all by 30 and will have to start all over again.

額

Protruding Forehead
凸額

As opposed to the Receding Forehead, the Protruding Forehead extends slightly outwards as viewed from the side profile.

If the protrusion is more prominent on the top of the forehead, this person can be described as serious, well-mannered and has a good sense of foresight. If the protrusion combines with a low and narrow forehead, this person is likely to show courage without much thought.

This feature also denotes that the person tends to be an analyzer. At times, he or she tends to over-analyze matters and hence, becoming indecisive.

額,頰,頦

35

Flat Forehead
直額

When the forehead is straight up with no angle and is not rounded, it suggests the Straight Forehead.

People with such foreheads are logical and linear thinking or considered as sequential thinkers. They are unable to accept information that are presented too fast or in a disorderly manner, and prefers it to be delivered step-by-step accordingly.

They require time to assimilate things and thus, do not appreciate being forced to give immediate response. They do not handle pressure well and may become overwhelmed and eventually shut down. However, their strength is when they learn something new they tend to retain it in their mind for a long time.

额，颡，颏

Wide Forehead 寬闊額

A person who has a Wide or Broad Forehead refers to a forehead that has a distance larger than usual from side to side.

A Wide or Broad Forehead is preferable, especially if it also come with good Qi complexion or color that is bright or with a natural glow. Strong, broad foreheads are also indicative of high IQ levels, which is why such foreheads are commonly seen on successful entrepreneurs and corporate figures. People with Wide Foreheads are capable of executing their work diligently and tend to make good mentors due to their helpful nature. This forehead is also commonly seen on well-respected individuals or those in the high society.

There must not be any presence of bumps, scars or lines crossing the Life, Career, Traveling and Parents Palaces on the forehead as well as this will affect the pertinent aspects indicated by the Palaces.

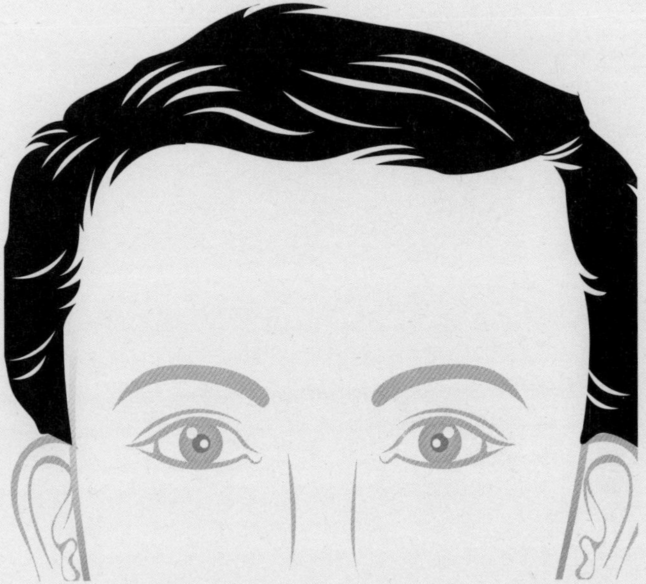

額　顏　顱

Forehead with Narrow Bottom and Wider Top
下窄上寬額

A Forehead with Narrow Bottom and Wider Top refers to the hairline area being wider than the bottom part of the forehead towards the eyebrows.

A Forehead with a Narrow Bottom tends to affect the Marriage or Life Palace, which is located between the outer tips of the eyebrows and the ears on both sides of the face. This is especially so if the bottom part also happens to be sunken and bony. With such circumstances, a person with this forehead is not blessed with good relationship luck with his or her spouse. They tend to lack passion and trust in the relationship.

Conversely, a tall, wide and full forehead is good for entrepreneurs and business people. It's a sign of good networking skills and the ability to get along well with others. They tend to enjoy better career luck due to their higher Intelligence (IQ) and Emotional Quotients (EQ).

額，頰

Peaked Hairline

This is where the hairline rises to a point toward the crown of the head, which looks like the tip of a flame.

The Peaked Hairline signifies grand ambition and a desire to rise to greater heights. People with this hairline have great intelligence but, on the down side, be markedly intolerant of other people's views and is stubbornly fixed in his own.

This hairline combined with a high forehead refers to an ambitious person with the will to succeed. On the other hand, those with a low forehead tend to be impractical and immature in their thinking, and will likely daydream of their success than putting in the effort for it.

A person with the Peaked Hairline also wishes to put a lot of distance between himself and his origins by re-creating a life in his own terms.

額，顙，頟

Rounded Hairline

The Rounded Hairline refers to a neatly curved hairline with no jagged edge. It is also considered a watery hair growth pattern.

If this hairline is combined with other face shapes, then it will indicate a person with a powerful intuition and a more open expression of feeling.

As Water is a changeable element, this person is possibly someone fickle-minded. If this hairline is coupled with a Water face shape – which is either round or chubby faced, or irregular in shape - then it denotes a superstitious and overly imaginative character.

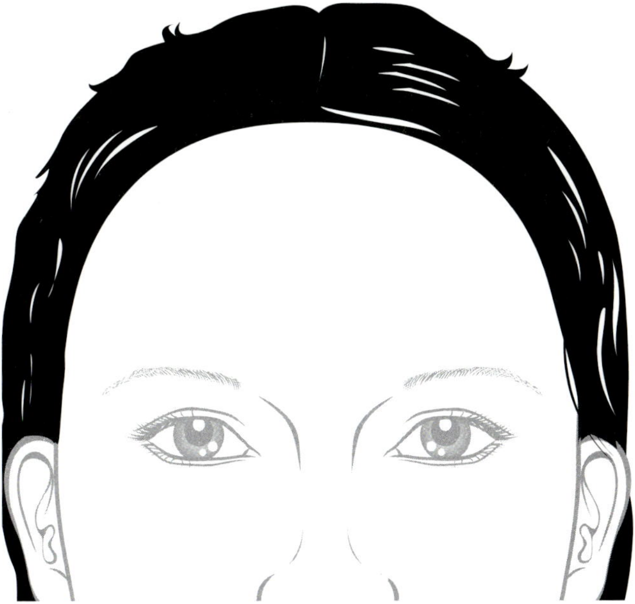

額，顙，頲

45

Brow Ridge

The Brow Ridge refers to the bony ridge or supraorbital torus, a protruding ridge above the eye sockets.

This indicates a person who prefers the right or proven answers and may feel immobilized if the rules are not followed. People with such ridge tend to be conservative and by-the-book in what they do.

A person with a prominent Brow Ridge may also be perceived as stern, which probably works well in terms of leadership, since they have a no-nonsense and military-type approach, and the tendency to pursue every rule to the letter and expect others to follow suit. In other words, they are likely to be rigid and inflexible, and may have difficulty in accepting changes.

額

No Brow Ridge

As the name suggests, this refers to the lack of a bony ridge above the eye sockets.

It denotes a flexible, adaptable and spontaneous approach with the ability to accept new ideas. People with No Brow Ridge seek whatever is needed in the moment and will use what works best for now without looking too far to the future or its consequences.

They also tend to avoid being overly technical and resents being forced to be too detailed or rigid in their approach. In that sense, they may appear flaky and flighty when pressed to stick to the rules.

額，顙

Self-Will Pad

This pad refers to the fleshy – not fatty - bump that appears on the space between the two eyebrows, which makes it look rather "padded". It is also the focal point of a person's mental sense of self.

As the area between the eyebrows signifies self-will, when this feature is prominent, it means that this person has a tremendous innate self-will and can accomplish goals by the force of will and sheer determination. Once they have made up their minds, nothing can stand in their way to sway it.

With a natural-born determination and steadfast spirit, people with such feature are able to hold onto their position at times of adversity or even when under pressure.

額、顛、頯

51

Cheeks

Large Cheeks 大臉頰

A person with Large Cheeks has fleshy or plump cheeks. This person is likely to have high cheekbones as well.

This belongs to those who are capable of wielding power well. They have great presence and charisma that can command the respect of others.

People with Large Cheeks have good leadership, organizational and people skills, which makes them manager-material due to their ability to monitor their staff efficiently and effectively.

額，顙也

Small Cheeks
小臉頰

Small Cheeks are defined as recessed or sunken and less ample in flesh compared to those with Large Cheeks.

As high cheekbones denote good leadership, people with Small Cheeks seem to fall short in possessing the requisite strength, authority and power to keep things in proper order. Therefore, they have a poor presence and are likely the ones with difficulty earning the attention and respect of others.

However, they may be able to manage people better by being stricter, and rewarding those who stood by them.

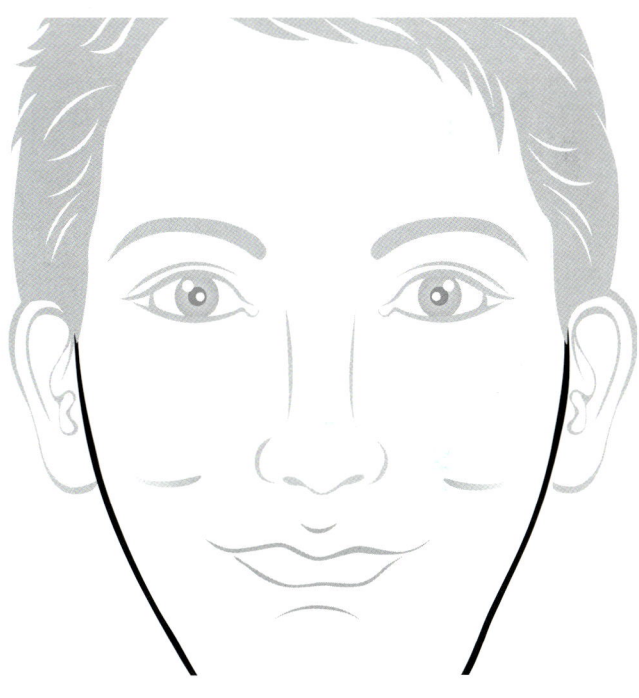

额,颜,颏

Wide Cheeks 寬臉頰

Wide Cheeks refer to cheeks that are set far apart and with wide cheekbones

It reflects a person who can go the distance because of his or her long-term stamina and endurance, which also tends to wear out most people who try to keep up with them. Quitting is not an option. Such people are known for their great personal power and a can-do attitude.

This feature is considered ideal for women because it denotes that they have a higher ability to protect themselves and vigilant. They have a sense not to cross anyone without any justification.

Outward Growing Cheeks 外凸臉頰

Outward Growing Cheeks refer to those that point away from the center of the face.

People with these cheeks tend to be extroverts. They are those who are able to express themselves and share their feelings more easily. They are go-getters and enjoy being the center of the attention.

They thrive in social settings and tend to have a large network of friends and acquaintances.

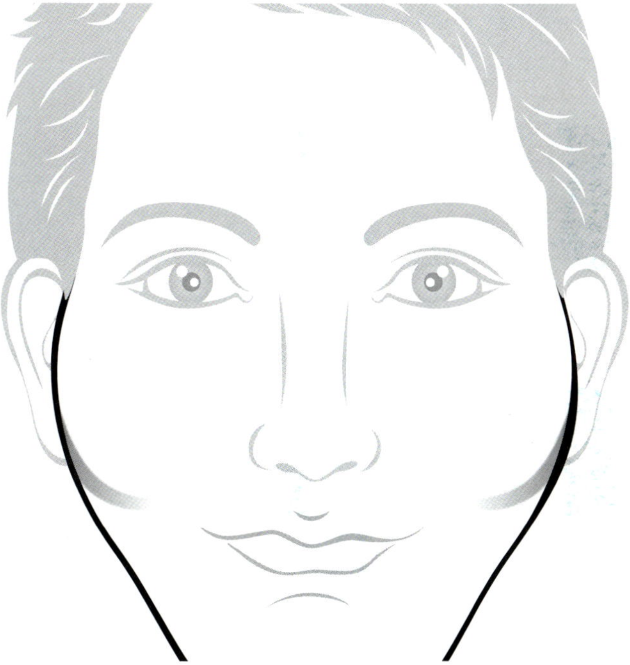

額、顙

Inward Growing Cheeks 内凸頰

Inward Growing Cheeks refer to those that point toward the interior of the center of the face.

This signifies an introvert, a person who prefers to keep their thoughts and feelings to themselves, or share them only with close and trusted friends and loved ones.

They tend to have a shy nature and are not at ease in social settings that require them to mingle around. They are not confrontational and prefer to stay in a low profile.

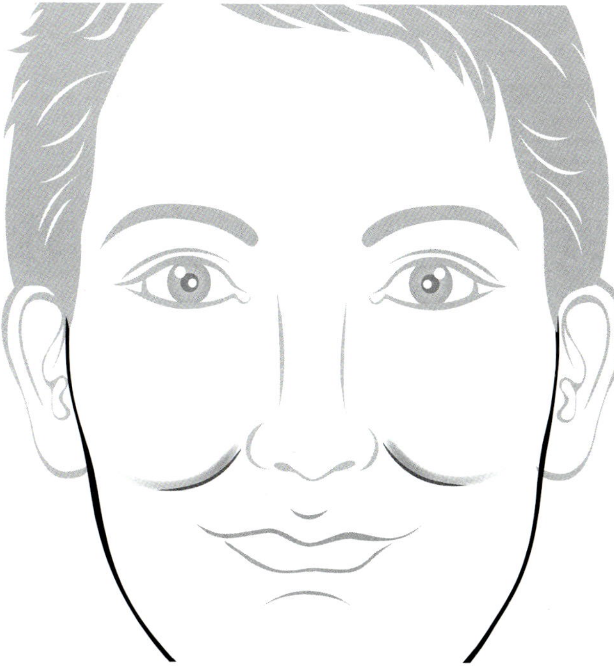

额

Line Growing Across Cheeks
破顴紋

This feature refers to a line or lines that appear across either one or both of the cheeks.

Lines that cut across Positions 46 and 47 – which are the cheekbones on the face signify a removal of power, wealth or authority. People with such lines in this positions may be rich and successful, but risk losing whatever material achievements they've gained towards their middle life. This is especially so if it is coupled with an unfavorable nose type from the Face Reading perspective.

Individuals with these lines also tend to be paranoid about their children and could possibly be over-controlling of their offspring.

額、顏、頟

65

Stolen Spouse Mole
妻奪夫權痣

This mole is located directly below the eye in the center of the cheek, either on the right or left side. The presence of this mole indicates that a person who is likely to lose their boyfriend, girlfriend or spouse to a third party despite being in a long term relationship. Hence, it is named the Stolen Spouse Mole.

A person with a Stolen Spouse Mole will not find good fortune in terms of romance, especially in the case of a love triangle, where he or she will likely be the losing party.

Career-wise, this mole position also indicates the possibility of losing control or authority over something he or she owns, such as a job or business.

Healer Cheeks

The Healer Cheeks are broadest at both sides of the face, besides the eyes.

It is named so as it denotes an individual with an aura of nurturing, healing and uplifting energy. Thus, signs of a natural healer. People with Healer Cheeks have a special gift, a natural ability to uplift and encourage others.

Suitable careers include doctors, nurses, psychologists, counselors, massage therapists, and teachers. They also make good parents.

額、顴、頦

High cheekbones
高顴骨

High Cheekbones refer to cheekbones that appear high and imposing, and appear somewhat prominent.

People with High Cheekbones tend to be positive-minded and action-oriented people who like challenges. They typically do not shy from adventure and tend to go forth and attack a particular task or project instead of waiting for an opportunity to come to him.

If the High Cheekbones are combined with particularly sharp features, as well as a face with sharp angles, then the individual is likely to be somewhat arrogant. In extreme situations, people with this combination of features can betray people close to them in order to achieve a goal.

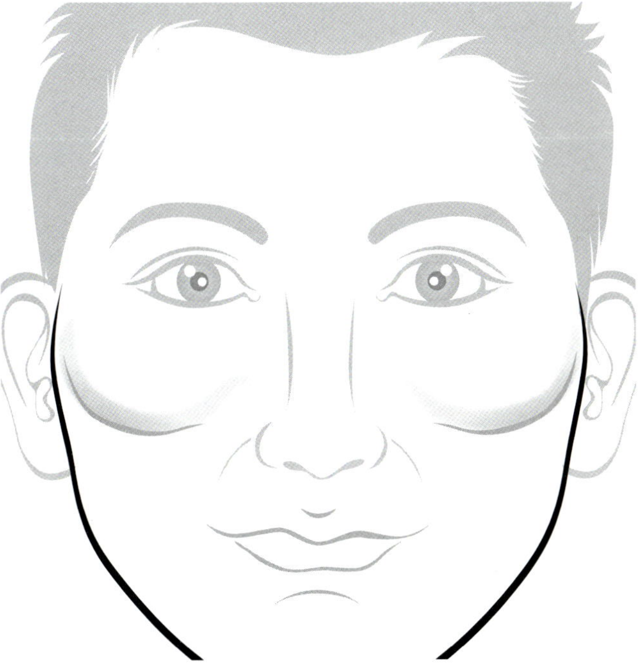

額，顙

Low cheekbones
低顴骨

Low Cheekbones denote cheekbones that settle lower in the face, and are not very prominent.

Individuals with Low Cheekbones tend to be somewhat timid people who lack courage and a sense of competition. They tend to be a little passive in their approach to the world.

People with this type of cheekbones are also exceptionally tolerant and gentle, as they always try to accommodate others. They can also be indecisive and lack motivation and drive, and may rely on others to get things going. This can prove to be a disadvantage in social networks and interpersonal relationships, and they can be easily taken for granted by others because of this.

額,顴

Thin Cheekbones
薄顴骨

Thin Cheekbones are cheekbones that appear lean and somewhat delicate, as opposed to broad and strong.

Individuals with Thin Cheekbones tend to have a poor constitution, and their physical health may be weak. In terms of mental constitution, as well, people with Thin Cheekbones tend to feel sad easily, and lonely. They lack the competitive spirit and may also suffer from inauspicious luck.

Women with Thin Cheekbones tend to have even lower competitive drives, and may easily be pushed around by men. They tend to have a conservative, close-minded mindset and may be easily anxious or nervous. They lack family warmth and security, and health-wise they also have a bad digestive system.

額，顙、頟

Orange Peel Cheeks
顴如桔皮

Orange Peel Cheeks refer to cheeks where the skin is rough and grainy, like orange peel.

People with Orange Peel Cheeks tend to be the kind of people who can never sit still. They tend to be running around, taking care of other people's business as well as their own! As such, they rarely know a moment's rest.

Their luck tends to take a dip during their years of middle-age, as their life is prone to instability during those years. There is the likelihood for men to become easily lonely, while married women might betray their spouse easily.

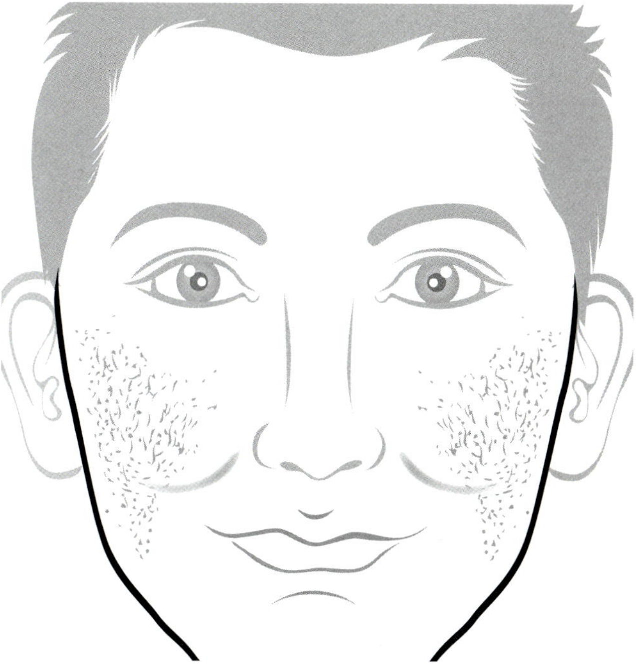

額、瀕、頷

77

Pimple on the Cheek
顴上生瘡

Pimple on the Cheek denotes a pimple or blemish on either one of the cheeks.

The presence of a pimple on the cheek denotes poor luck in fulfilling one's goals, as the person is likely to find it harder to complete what one is doing. There will be obstructions and blocks that prevent a smooth path.

If one has an important goal to fulfill, it might be best to wait until the pimple disappears. While the pimple is present, it will not be advisable to make important decisions as pertaining to house moving, job change, or even potential travel.

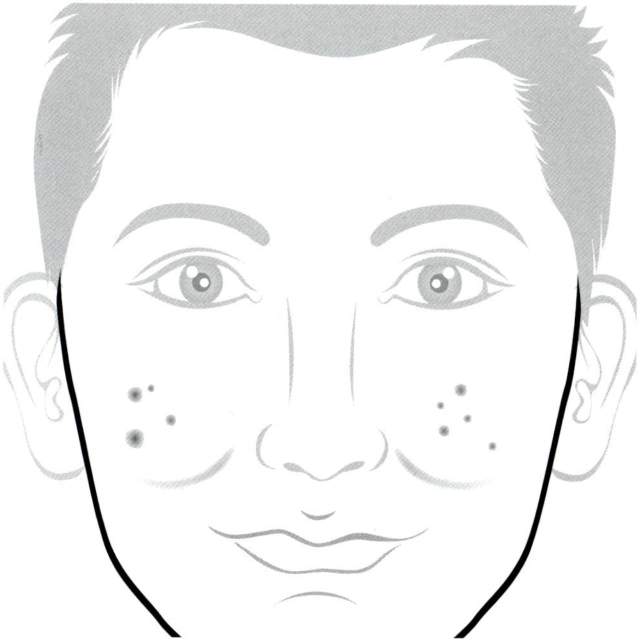

額、頰、顏

Mole on Cheeks
顴生黑痣

If a mole appears on both cheeks, and is fairly prominent and black in colour and tone, this is actually a good thing – as it denotes that the individual is likely to possess authority.

If the mole appears only on one cheek, it indicates a useful situation at work where one's boss or superior is likely to have high hopes and great trust in one's ability to fulfill a task or get the job done. As such, a mole on one cheek denotes help and trust from the higher-ups, and it also indicates the likelihood of popularity in social occasions.

If the mole appears dull and grey, the individual is likely to be afraid of heights. As such, activities that involve heights, like mountain climbing, are not recommended. Similarly, it also denotes a greater risk of heart attacks.

額，顴，頦

81

Chin

Large Chin 巨頦

A Large Chin represents a strong and well-defined chin.

People with such chins are assertive, competitive and aggressive in nature. They have a survivor's instinct and great perseverance that can weather through any challenges in life.

They tend to ooze confidence in what they do. However, such strong characteristics may – on the flip side - make them seem intimidating or antagonistic to others.

Small Chin 小頦

A Small Chin refers to people with a delicate chin that does not appear prominent enough on the face or is relatively smaller compared to a normal-sized chin.

People with Small Chins have a modest persona as opposed to those with Large Chins. They are sensitive to criticism and overwhelming life experiences. They tend to be hard on themselves and can be unassertive when faced with criticism.

They are also not aggressive and non-competitive, and rely on the encouragement and support from others to help them through tough times in life.

額，顴，頦

Long Chin 長頦

The Long Chin refers to a chin where the distance between the teeth and the tip of the chin is exceptionally long.

People with Long Chins reflect well-grounded individuals with an innate physical power. They are also knowledgeable and trustworthy in nature.

They tend to consider their thoughts thoroughly before they make any final decisions. They are more analytical and meticulous, and do not act rash or impulsive in any situations.

额
颊 颏

89

Double Chin 雙下巴

A Double Chin denotes the subcutaneous fat around the neck that sags down and creates the appearance of a second 'chin'. Although it is common to assume that only people who are overweight bears the Double Chin, the elderly and those with average weight may also have this feature.

The Double Chin is a positive feature to have when one reaches his or her senior years. It represents a good and happy old age with plenty of people to take care of its possessor and to keep him or her company.

Double-chinned individuals will enjoy prosperity and good support from family members and friends in their old age.

額,顙,頟

Protruding Chin 凸頦

A Protruding Chin is when the chin sticks out as seen from the side.

People with Protruding Chins are formidable adversary who does not get easily intimidated or bluffed. They usually get the last word in any discussion or argument.

Never a quitter, they do not shy away from challenges and rarely do anything midway – even in relationships. They also have a difficulty of letting things go easily and tend to hold onto them for a long as possible.

Receding Chin
後縮頦

A Receding Chin refers to a chin that recedes or a weak chin that slopes posteriorly instead of outwards.

This is generally an unfavorable chin as it indicates a person with a lower-than-average IQ level. People with Receding Chins tend to be non-committal and are likely to leave many things unfinished midway.

In addition, such chin does not bode well for the person in his or her old age. Upon reaching the age of sixty, people with this chin will not have anyone to take care of them and their latter years will likely be a lonely one.

額,顴

Rounded Chin
圓頦

This refers to a chin that is nicely rounded without angles.

People with Rounded Chin are believed to be friendly, warm, open-hearted and emotional in character. They are known to be able to make the best of any situation, are at ease with themselves and the world around them, and have a charming nature. They are never aggressive or harsh.

If this feature combines with a longer and more prominent chin, such people will use their charm to their own advantage, especially in winning friends over and influencing people.

額、顎、頸

Square Chin 方頦

A Square Chin is angular and looks flat on the bottom with a noticeably squared-off shape.

Square-chinned people are hardworking, and have considerable self-will and high achievement. They don't give up easily and are known to challenge problems head-on. They have the ability to point out the pros and cons of any issues, which makes them a great consultant and debater.

They are trustworthy, honorable and steadfast in all forms of partnership, and tend to be honest and straight-forward in their dealings. Though they possess deep, strong feelings, they tend to lack charm and at times, take the fun out of things due to their fierce competitive nature.

頷 頜 頸

99

Straight Chin
直頦

A Straight Chin is one that neither recedes nor protrudes and appears straight from the side profile.

People with Straight Chins are idealistic individuals. They are highly motivated by causes and ideas that they believe in and tend to go all out in their actions.

They have a balanced approach towards commitment and can be counted on to get the job done. Though they do not quit easily or do anything midway, they have the good sense to know when it is time to give up if the circumstances call for it.

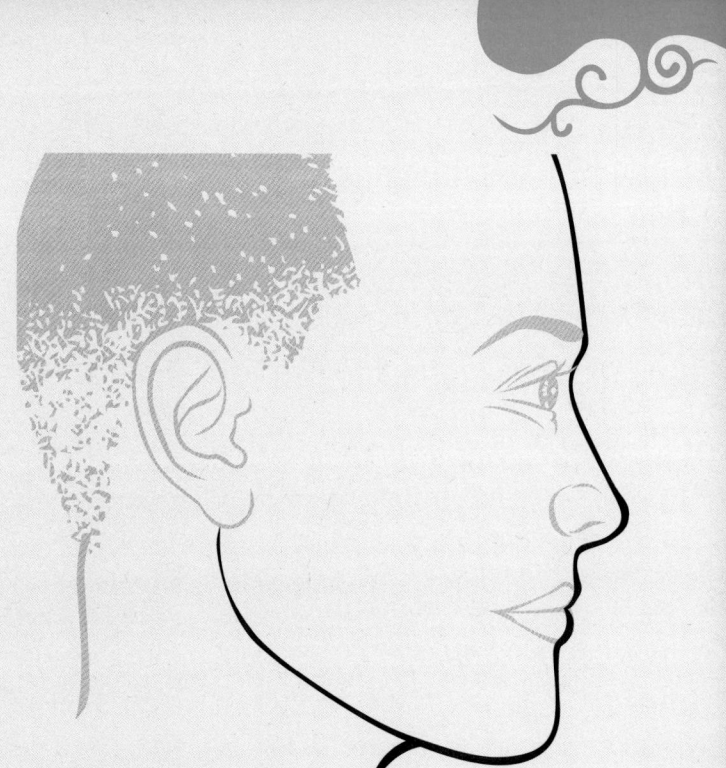

額,顴,頦

101

Cleft Chin 酒渦在下巴

This is a variant of the Square Chin which is dimpled or has a cleft on it. It is a Y-shaped fissure on the chin that follows the fissure of the lower jaw bone.

The Cleft Chin is a sign of a playful nature. People with such chins will remain youthful even in their old age, but needs to be loved.

This feature is commonly found on people who are very creative, innovative and artistic in nature.

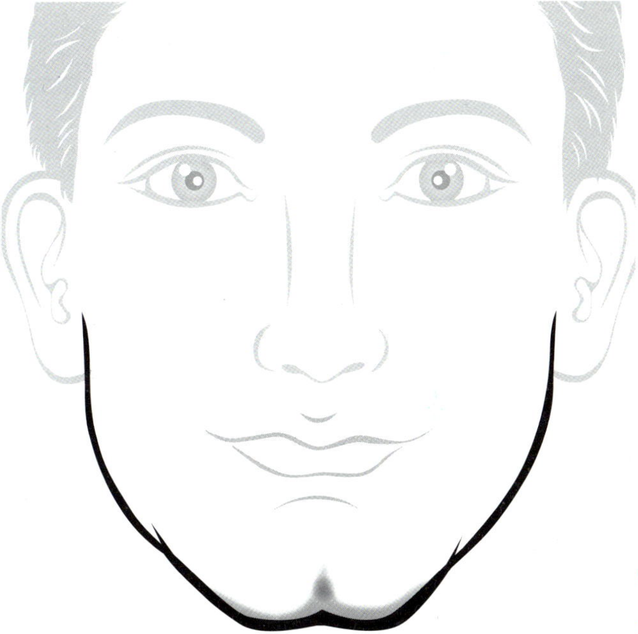

額,顎,頦

103

Jutting, Broad Chin
寬頦

A chin that is broad and jutting shares similarities in attributes and traits with the Square Chin. However, the shape of this chin extends the qualities of inner strength and honor.

The negative qualities of this chin indicate a person who is pushy, a charismatic flirt and an attractive charmer with a possibility of being an unfaithful partner.

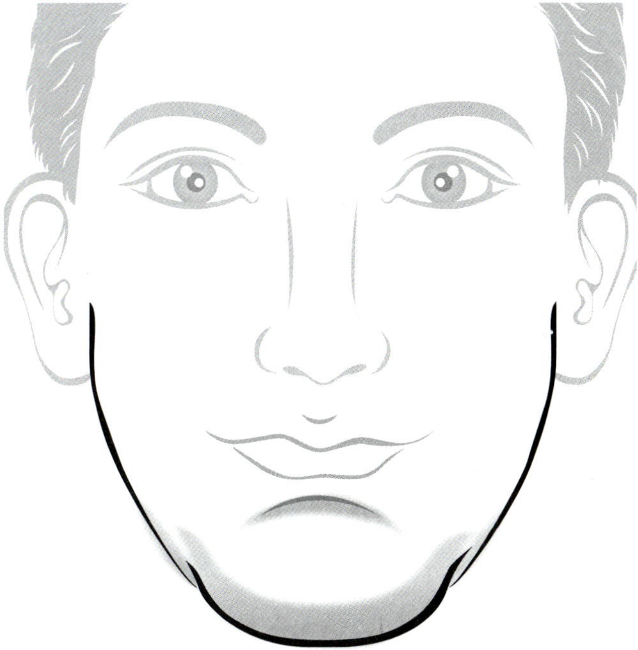

額，顴，頦

Pointed, Narrow Chin
尖頦

This refers to a chin that is pointed in its edge and not broad, but narrow.

People with a chin that is both pointed and narrow are considered weak-minded and have a less attractive personality. Such people will always be plagued with depression. They tend to lack willpower and because of this also tend to be plagued by unfulfilled hopes and dreams.

In ancient China, this feature was believed to indicate loneliness, betrayal and the likelihood of a short life.

額，顴瘦

Arch on Chin

This "arch" is a curved line across the center of the chin. It is almost similar to the Cleft Chin, but forms a deeper and curvy arch.

The arch on the chin denotes people who need to seek affirmation of their self-worth from others. This stems from a childhood that lacks attention and appreciation, which eventually leads to a low self-esteem.

As such, how they feel about themselves can be changeable and highly contingent on the feedback they receive from others on any given day.

額，顏，頤

Chin with Bumpy Appearance

As the name explains, this denotes a chin with an uneven appearance due to quite a few bumps on it that mars its smoothness.

This type of bumpy chin denotes people who have hardened themselves to meet perpetual difficulties in life. They are ever-ready to face adversity, and can be tough and obstinate when challenged.

These are not people who give up easily when faced with a wall or an obstruction, and hence can also be somewhat forward-thinking.

額、顎、頬

Oval shape 橢圓型

This denotes a chin that when seen from the front possesses an oval shape.

People with oval chins tend be elegant and sensitive individuals, but because of this they can be dull and somewhat reticent in personal relationships. They tend to lack courage and can have a hard time making up their mind and coming to a decision.

Women with an oval-shaped chin tend to be creative, artistic types with a great passion and zest for life. In matters of romance, once she decides to love or be with someone, she will do so with the intention of being with the person until the end.

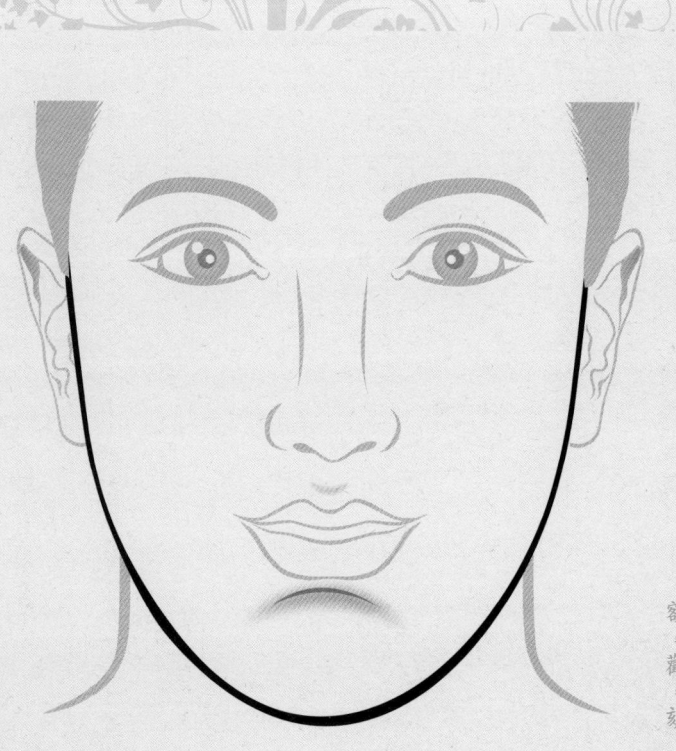

額,顙,頏

Square Shape 四方型

This denotes a chin that appears even and square-shaped when seen from the front.

If a man has a square-shaped chin, he is likely to be of stocky physical build, and with lots of reserves of energy. He will most likely be a determined person who approaches matters rationally, and will be faithful in love. However, this is if the chin is fleshy. If it's square-shaped and bony or angular, the man is likely to be irrational, and prone to being uncouth and rude.

A woman with a square-shaped chin may be assertive and very capable in her work.

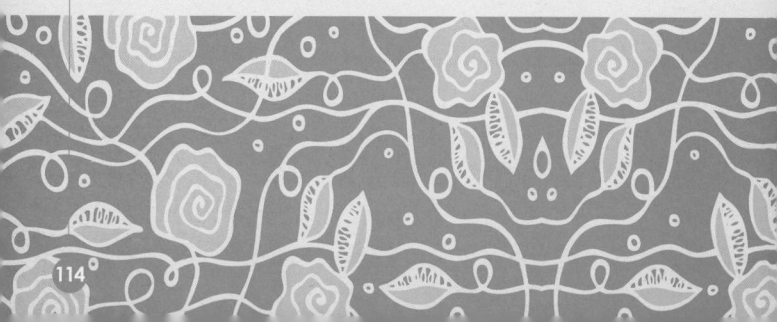

Scoop Shape 畚斗型

A scoop-shaped chin denotes a chin that appears round, and bears a somewhat 'stretched' appearance towards the front.

People with this type of chin tend to be very creative, and they possess original and fresh thoughts. As such, most people with a scoop-shaped chin tend to be artistic or those who work or dabble in artistic fields.

They also tend to be the sort that is forward-thinking and keen on moving ahead with something, and as such are more than likely to be overly ambitious.

額，顴，頦

About Joey Yap

Joey Yap first began learning about Chinese Metaphysics from masters in the field when he was fifteen.

Despite having graduated with a Commerce degree in Accounting, Joey never became an accountant. Instead, he began to give seminars, talks and professional Chinese Metaphysic consultations in Malaysia, Singapore, India, Australia, Canada, England, Germany and the United States, becoming a household name in the field.

By the age of twenty-six, Joey became a self-made millionaire and in 2008, he was listed in The Malaysian Tatler as the Top 300 Most Influential People in Malaysia and Prestige's Top 40 Under 40.

His practical and result-driven take on Feng Shui and BaZi sets him apart from other older, traditional masters and practitioners in the field. He shows people how the ancient teachings can be utilized for tangible REAL world benefits. The success he and his clients enjoy, thanks to his advice, is positive proof that Feng Shui and BaZi Astrology works, whether everyone believes in it or not!

Today, Joey has helped and worked with governments and the wealthiest people in Singapore, Hong Kong, China, Malaysia and Japan. His clients include multinationals, developers, tycoons and royalties. On Bloomberg, he is featured on-air as a regular guest on the subject of Feng Shui annual forecasts. He is retained by twenty-five top Malaysian property developers to help determine suitable candidates to take top management, change their space and Feng Shui mechanism, the way they make decisions, and understand the natural cosmic energies that can influence their decision-making.

Every year he conducts his 'Feng Shui and Astrology' seminar to a crowd of more than 3500 people at the Kuala Lumpur Convention Center. He also takes this annual seminar on a world tour to Frankfurt, San Francisco, New York, Las Vegas, Toronto, Sydney and Singapore.

The Joey Yap Consulting Group is the world's largest and first specialized metaphysics consultation firm. His consultancy, and professional speaking and training engagements with Microsoft, HP, Bloomberg, Citibank, HSBC and many more have seen the benefits of Classical Feng Shui and BaZi find their way into corporate environment and culture. Celebrities, property developers and other large organizations turn to Joey when they need the best.

After years of field-testing and fine-tuning his teachings, he has put together a team in the form of Joey Yap Research International. The objective of this Research Team is to scientifically track and verify the positive impact of Feng Shui and BaZi on subjects and ultimately to assist more people in achieving their life goals.

The Mastery Academy of Chinese Metaphysics which Joey founded teaches thousands of students from all around the world about Classical Feng Shui, Chinese Astrology and Face Reading. Many graduates have gone on to become successful in their own right, becoming sought after consultants, setting up their own consultancy businesses or even becoming educators, passing on Chinese Metaphysics knowledge to others.

Joey has also created the Decision Referential Technology™, offering decision reformation training on how to make better decisions in business and in personal life. He has led his team of highly trained consultants to help clients create more positive change in corporate boardrooms and increase production in their companies, helping people see their business outlook for each year so they may anticipate, plan and execute their strategies successfully.

Joey's work has been featured regularly in various popular global publications and networks like Time, Forbes, the International Herald Tribune and Bloomberg. He has also written columns for The New Straits Times, The Star and The Edge – Malaysia's leading newspapers. He has achieved bestselling author status with over sixty-five books, which have sold more than three million copies to-date.

His success is not limited to matters of Feng Shui and BaZi. Although his success is a product of them, he is also a successful entrepreneur, leading his own companies and property investment portfolio. When not teaching metaphysics or consulting around the world, Joey is a Naruto-fan, avid snowboarder and is crazy for fruits de mer.

Author's personal website :

www.joeyyap.com

Joey Yap on Facebook:

www.facebook.com/JoeyYapFB

MASTERY ACADEMY
OF CHINESE METAPHYSICS
Your **Preferred** Choice to the Art & Science of Classical Chinese Metaphysics Studies

Bringing **innovative** techniques and **creative** teaching methods to an ancient study.

Mastery Academy of Chinese Metaphysics was established by Joey Yap to play the role of disseminating this Eastern knowledge to the modern world with the belief that this valuable knowledge should be accessible to anyone, anywhere.

Its goal is to enrich people's lives through accurate, professional teaching and practice of Chinese Metaphysics knowledge globally. It is the first academic institution of its kind in the world to adopt the tradition of Western institutions of higher learning - where students are encourage to explore, question and challenge themselves and to respect different fields and branches of study - with the appreciation and respect of classical ideas and applications that have stood the test of time.

The art and science of Chinese Metaphysics studies – be it Feng Shui, BaZi (Astrology), Mian Xiang (Face Reading), ZeRi (Date Selection) or Yi Jing – is no longer a field shrouded with mystery and superstition. In light of new technology, fresher interpretations and innovative methods as well as modern teaching tools like the Internet, interactive learning, e-learning and distance learning, anyone from virtually any corner of the globe, who is keen to master these disciplines can do so with ease and confidence under the guidance and support of the Academy.

It has indeed proven to be a center of educational excellence for thousands of students from over thirty countries across the world; many of whom have moved on to practice classical Chinese Metaphysics professionally in their home countries.

At the Academy, we believe in enriching people's lives by empowering their destinies through the disciplines of Chinese Metaphysics. Learning is not an option - it's a way of life!

MALAYSIA
19-3, The Boulevard, Mid Valley City, 59200 Kuala Lumpur, Malaysia
Tel : +603-2284 8080 | Fax : +603-2284 1218
Email   : info@masteryacademy.com
Website : www.masteryacademy.com

Australia, Austria, Canada, China, Croatia, Cyprus, Czech Republic, Denmark, France, Germany, Greece, Hungary, India, Italy, Kazakhstan, Malaysia, Netherlands (Holland), New Zealand, Philippines, Poland, Russian Federation, Singapore, Slovenia, South Africa, Switzerland, Turkey, U.S.A., Ukraine, United Kingdom

www.masteryacademy.com | +603 - 2284 8080

Mastery Academy around the world

JOEY YAP CONSULTING GROUP

Pioneering Metaphysics - Centric Personal Coaching and Corporate Consulting

The Joey Yap Consulting Group is the world's first specialised metaphysics consultation firm. Founded in 2002 by renown international Feng Shui and BaZi consultant, author and trainer Joey Yap, the Joey Yap Consulting Group is a pioneer in the provision of metaphysics-driven coaching and consultation services for individuals and corporations.

The Group's core consultation practice areas are Feng Shui and BaZi, which are complimented by ancillary services like Date Selection, Face Reading and Yi Jing Divination. The Group's team of highly-trained professional consultants are led by Principal Consultant Joey Yap. The Joey Yap Consulting Group is the firm of choice for corporate captains, entrepreneurs, celebrities and property developers when it comes to Feng Shui and BaZi-related advisory and knowledge.

Across Industries: Our Portfolio of Clients

Our diverse portfolio of both corporate and individual clients from all around the world bears testimony to our experience and capabilities.

Joey Yap Consulting Group is the firm of choice for many of Asia's leading multi-national corporations, listed entities, conglomerates and top-tier property developers when it comes to Feng Shui and corporate BaZi.

Our services also engaged by professionals, prominent business personalities, celebrities, high-profile politicians and people from all walks of life.

JOEY YAP CONSULTING GROUP

Name (Mr./Mrs./Ms.): _____

Contact Details

Tel: _____ Fax: _____

Mobile: _____

E-mail: _____

What Type of Consultation Are You Interested In?
☐ Feng Shui ☐ BaZi ☐ Date Selection ☐ Corporate Events

Please tick if applicable:
☐ Are you a Property Developer looking to engage Joey Yap Consulting Group?

☐ Are you a Property Investor looking for tailor-made packages to suit your investment requirements?

Please attach your name card here.

Thank you for completing this form. Please fax it back to us at:

Malaysia & the rest of the world
Fax : +603-2284 2213 Tel : +603-2284 1213

www.joeyyap.com

Feng Shui Consultations

For Residential Properties
- Initial Land/Property Assessment
- Residential Feng Shui Consultations
- Residential Land Selection
- End-to-End Residential Consultation

For Commercial Properties
- Initial Land/Property Assessment
- Commercial Feng Shui Consultations
- Commercial Land Selection
- End-to-End Commercial Consultation

For Property Developers
- End-to-End Consultation
- Post-Consultation Advisory Services
- Panel Feng Shui Consultant

For Property Investors
- Your Personal Feng Shui Consultant
- Tailor-Made Packages

For Memorial Parks & Burial Sites
- Yin House Feng Shui

BaZi Consultations

Personal Destiny Analysis
- Personal Destiny Analysis for Individuals
- Children's BaZi Analysis
- Family BaZi Analysis

Strategic Analysis for Corporate Organizations
- Corporate BaZi Consultations
- BaZi Analysis for Human Resource Management

Entrepreneurs & Business Owners
- BaZi Analysis for Entrepreneurs

Career Pursuits
- BaZi Career Analysis

Relationships
- Marriage and Compatibility Analysis
- Partnership Analysis

For Everyone
- Annual BaZi Forecast
- Your Personal BaZi Coach

Date Selection Consultations

- Marriage Date Selection
- Caesarean Birth Date Selection
- House-Moving Date Selection
- Renovation & Groundbreaking Dates
- Signing of Contracts
- Official Openings
- Product Launches

Corporate Events

Many reputable organizations and instituitions have worked closely with Joey Yap Consulting Group to build a synergistic business relationship by engaging our team of consultants, led by Joey Yap, as speakers at their corporate events.

We tailor our seminars and talks to suit the anticipated or pertinent group of audience. Be it department, subsidiary, your clients or even the entire corporation, we aim to fit your requirements in delivering the intended message(s).

Tel: +603-2284 1213   Email: consultation@joeyyap.com

CHINESE METAPHYSICS REFERENCE SERIES

The Chinese Metaphysics Reference Series is a collection of reference texts, source material, and educational textbooks to be used as supplementary guides by scholars, students, researchers, teachers and practitioners of Chinese Metaphysics.

These comprehensive and structured books provide fast, easy reference to aid in the study and practice of various Chinese Metaphysics subjects including Feng Shui, BaZi, Yi Jing, Zi Wei, Liu Ren, Ze Ri, Ta Yi, Qi Men and Mian Xiang.

The Chinese Metaphysics Compendium

At over 1,000 pages, the *Chinese Metaphysics Compendium* is a unique one-volume reference book that compiles all the formulas relating to Feng Shui, BaZi (Four Pillars of Destiny), Zi Wei (Purple Star Astrology), Yi Jing (I-Ching), Qi Men (Mystical Doorways), Ze Ri (Date Selection), Mian Xiang (Face Reading) and other sources of Chinese Metaphysics.

It is presented in the form of easy-to-read tables, diagrams and reference charts, all of which are compiled into one handy book. This first-of-its-kind compendium is presented in both English and the original Chinese, so that none of the meanings and contexts of the technical terminologies are lost.

The only essential and comprehensive reference on Chinese Metaphysics, and an absolute must-have for all students, scholars, and practitioners of Chinese Metaphysics.

| The Ten Thousand Year Calendar (Pocket Edition) | The Ten Thousand Year Calendar | Dong Gong Date Selection | The Date Selection Compendium | Plum Blossoms Divination Reference Book | San Yuan Dragon Gate Eight Formations Water Method | Xuan Kong Da Gua Ten Thousand Year Calendar |

| Bazi Hour Pillar Useful Gods - Wood | Bazi Hour Pillar Useful Gods - Fire | Bazi Hour Pillar Useful Gods - Earth | Bazi Hour Pillar Useful Gods - Metal | Bazi Hour Pillar Useful Gods - Water | Xuan Kong Da Gua Structures Reference Book | Xuan Kong Da Gua 64 Gua Transformation Analysis |

| Bazi Structures and Structural Useful Gods - Wood | Bazi Structures and Structural Useful Gods - Fire | Bazi Structures and Structural Useful Gods - Earth | Bazi Structures and Structural Useful Gods - Metal | Bazi Structures and Structural Useful Gods - Water | Xuan Kong Purple White Script | Earth Study Discern Truth Second Edition |

---

www.masteryacademy.com | +603 - 2284 8080

Joey Yap's BaZi Profiling System

Three Levels of BaZi Profiling (English & Chinese versions)

In BaZi Profiling, there are three levels that reflect three different stages of a person's personal nature and character structure.

Level 1 – The Day Master

The Day Master in a nutshell is the BASIC YOU. The inborn personality. It is your essential character. It answers the basic question "WHO AM I". There are ten basic personality profiles – the TEN Day Masters – each with its unique set of personality traits, likes and dislikes.

Level 2 – The Structure

The Structure is your behavior and attitude – in other words, how you use your personality. It expands on the Day Master (Level 1). The structure reveals your natural tendencies in life – are you more controlling, more of a creator, supporter, thinker or connector? Each of the Ten Day Masters express themselves differently through the FIVE Structures. Why do we do the things we do? Why do we like the things we like? – The answers are in our BaZi STRUCTURE.

Level 3 – The Profile

The Profile reveals your unique abilities and skills, the masks that you consciously and unconsciously "put on" as you approach and navigate the world. Your Profile speaks of your ROLES in life. There are TEN roles – or Ten BaZi Profiles. Everyone plays a different role.

What makes you happy and what does success mean to you is different to somebody else. Your sense of achievement and sense of purpose in life is unique to your Profile. Your Profile will reveal your unique style.

The path of least resistance to your success and wealth can only be accessed once you get into your "flow." Your BaZi Profile reveals how you can get FLOW. It will show you your patterns in work, relationship and social settings. Being AWARE of these patterns is your first step to positive Life Transformation.

www.baziprofiling.com

BaZi Collections

Leading Chinese Astrology Master Trainer Joey Yap makes it easy to learn how to unlock your Destiny through your BaZi with these books. BaZi or Four Pillars of Destiny is an ancient Chinese science which enables individuals to understand their personality, hidden talents and abilities as well as their luck cycle, simply by examining the information contained within their birth data.

Understand and appreciate more about this astoundingly accurate ancient Chinese Metaphysical science with this BaZi Collection.

Feng Shui Collection

Must-Haves for Property Analysis!

For homeowners, those looking to build their own home or even investors who are looking to apply Feng Shui to their homes, these series of books provides valuable information from the classical Feng Shui therioes and applications.

In his trademark straight-to-the-point manner, Joey shares with you the Feng Shui do's and dont's when it comes to finding a property with favorable Feng Shui, which is condusive for home living.

Stories & Lessons on Feng Shui Series

All in all, this series is a delightful chronicle of Joey's articles, thoughts and vast experience - as a professional Feng Shui consultant and instructor - that have been purposely refined, edited and expanded upon to make for a light-hearted, interesting yet educational read. And with Feng Shui, BaZi, Mian Xiang and Yi Jing all thrown into this one dish, there's something for everyone.

www.masteryacademy.com | +603 - 2284 8080

Continue Your Journey with Joey Yap Books in Feng Shui

Pure Feng Shui
Pure Feng Shui is Joey Yap's debut with an international publisher, CICO Books, and is a refreshing and elegant look at the intricacies of Classical Feng Shui – now compiled in a useful manner for modern-day readers. This book is a comprehensive introduction to all the important precepts and techniques of Feng Shui practice.

Your Aquarium Here
This book is the first in Fengshuilogy Series, a series of matter-in-fact and useful Feng Shui books designed for the person who wants to do a fuss-free Feng Shui.

Xuan Kong Flying Stars
This book is an essential introductory book to the subject of Xuan Kong Fei Xing, a well-known and popular system of Feng Shui. Learn 'tricks of the trade' and 'trade secrets' to enhance and maximize Qi in your home or office.

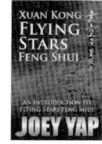

Walking the Dragons
Compiled in one book for the first time from Joey Yap's Feng Shui Mastery Excursion Series, the book highlights China's extensive, vibrant history with astute observations on the Feng Shui of important sites and places. Learn the landform formations of Yin Houses (tombs and burial places), as well as mountains, temples, castles, and villages.

The Art of Date Selection: Personal Date Selection
With the *Art of Date Selection: Personal Date Selection*, learn simple, practical methods you can employ to select not just good dates, but personalized good dates. Whether it's a personal activity such as a marriage or professional endeavor such as launching a business, signing a contract or even acquiring assets, this book will show you how to pick the good dates and tailor them to suit the activity in question, as well as avoid the negative ones too!

www.masteryacademy.com | +603 - 2284 8080

Face Reading Collection

Discover Face Reding (English & Chinese versions)

This is a comprehensive book on all areas of Face Reading, covering some of the most important facial features, including the forehead, mouth, ears and even philtrum above your lips. This book eill help you analyse not just your Destiny but help you achieve your full potential and achieve life fulfillment.

Joey Yap's Art of Face Reading

The Art of Face Reading is Joey Yap's second effort with CICO Books, and takes a lighter, more practical approach to Face Reading. This book does not so much focus on the individual features as it does on reading the entire face. It is about identifying common personality types and characters.

Easy Guide on Face Reading (English & Chinese versions)

The Face Reading Essentials series of books comprises 5 individual books on the key features of the face – Eyes, Eyebrows, Ears, Nose, and Mouth. Each book provides a detailed illustration and a simple yet descriptive explanation on the individual types of the features.

The books are equally useful and effective for beginners, enthusiasts, and the curious. The series is designed to enable people who are new to Face Reading to make the most of first impressions and learn to apply Face Reading skills to understand the personality and character of friends, family, co-workers, and even business associates.

Annual Releases
2011 Annual Outlook & Tong Shu

| Chinese Astrology for 2011 | Feng Shui for 2011 | Tong Shu Desktop Calendar 2011 | Professional Tong Shu Diary 2011 | Tong Shu Monthly Planner 2011 | Weekly Tong Shu Diary 2011 |

www.masteryacademy.com | +603 - 2284 8080

Educational Tools and Software

Xuan Kong Flying Stars Feng Shui Software
The Essential Application for Enthusiasts and Professionals

The Xuan Kong Flying Stars Feng Shui Software will assist you in the practice of Xuan Kong Feng Shui with minimum fuss and maximum effectiveness. Superimpose the Flying Stars charts over your house plans (or those of your clients) to clearly demarcate the 9 Palaces. Use it to help you create fast and sophisticated chart drawings and presentations, as well as to assist professional practitioners in the report-writing process before presenting the final reports for your clients. Students can use it to practice their Xuan Kong Feng Shui skills and knowledge, and it can even be used by designers and architects!

BaZi Ming Pan Software Version 2.0
Professional Four Pillars Calculator for Destiny Analysis

The BaZi Ming Pan Version 2.0 Professional Four Pillars Calculator for Destiny Analysis is the most technically advanced software of its kind in the world today. It allows even those without any knowledge of BaZi to generate their own BaZi Charts, and provides virtually every detail required to undertake a comprehensive Destiny Analysis.

This Professional Four Pillars Calculator allows you to even undertake a day-to-day analysis of your Destiny. What's more, all BaZi Charts generated by this software are fully printable and configurable! Designed for both enthusiasts and professional practitioners, this state-of-the-art software blends details with simplicity, and is capable of generating 4 different types of BaZi charts: **BaZi Professional Charts, BaZi Annual Analysis Charts, BaZi Pillar Analysis Charts and BaZi Family Relationship Charts.**

Joey Yap Feng Shui Template Set

Directions are the cornerstone of any successful Feng Shui audit or application. The **Joey Yap Feng Shui Template Set** is a set of three templates to simplify the process of taking directions and determining locations and positions, whether it's for a building, a house, or an open area such as a plot of land, all with just a floor plan or area map.

The Set comprises 3 basic templates: The Basic Feng Shui Template, 8 Mansions Feng Shui Template, and the Flying Stars Feng Shui Template.

Mini Feng Shui Compass

The Mini Feng Shui Compass is a self-aligning compass that is not only light at 100gms but also built sturdily to ensure it will be convenient to use anywhere. The rings on the Mini Feng Shui Compass are bi-lingual and incorporate the 24 Mountain Rings that is used in your traditional Luo Pan.

The comprehensive booklet included will guide you in applying the 24 Mountain Directions on your Mini Feng Shui Compass effectively and the 8 Mansions Feng Shui to locate the most auspicious locations within your home, office and surroundings. You can also use the Mini Feng Shui Compass when measuring the direction of your property for the purpose of applying Flying Stars Feng Shui.

www.masteryacademy.com | +603 - 2284 8080

Educational Tools and Software

Xuan Kong Vol.1
An Advanced Feng Shui Home Study Course

Learn the Xuan Kong Flying Star Feng Shui system in just 20 lessons! Joey Yap's specialised notes and course work have been written to enable distance learning without compromising on the breadth or quality of the syllabus. Learn at your own pace with the same material students in a live class would use. The most comprehensive distance learning course on Xuan Kong Flying Star Feng Shui in the market. Xuan Kong Flying Star Vol.1 comes complete with a special binder for all your course notes.

Feng Shui for Period 8 - (DVD)

Don't miss the Feng Shui Event of the next 20 years! Catch Joey Yap LIVE and find out just what Period 8 is all about. This DVD boxed set zips you through the fundamentals of Feng Shui and the impact of this important change in the Feng Shui calendar. Joey's entertaining, conversational style walks you through the key changes that Period 8 will bring and how to tap into Wealth Qi and Good Feng Shui for the next 20 years.

Xuan Kong Flying Stars Beginners Workshop - (DVD)

Take a front row seat in Joey Yap's Xuan Kong Flying Stars workshop with this unique LIVE RECORDING of Joey Yap's Xuan Kong Flying Stars Feng Shui workshop, attended by over 500 people. This DVD program provides an effective and quick introduction of Xuan Kong Feng Shui essentials for those who are just starting out in their study of classical Feng Shui. Learn to plot your own Flying Star chart in just 3 hours. Learn 'trade secret' methods, remedies and cures for Flying Stars Feng Shui. This boxed set contains 3 DVDs and 1 workbook with notes and charts for reference.

BaZi Four Pillars of Destiny Beginners Workshop - (DVD)

Ever wondered what Destiny has in store for you? Or curious to know how you can learn more about your personality and inner talents? BaZi or Four Pillars of Destiny is an ancient Chinese science that enables us to understand a person's hidden talent, inner potential, personality, health and wealth luck from just their birth data. This specially compiled DVD set of Joey Yap's BaZi Beginners Workshop provides a thorough and comprehensive introduction to BaZi. Learn how to read your own chart and understand your own luck cycle. This boxed set contains 3 DVDs and 1 workbook with notes and reference charts.

www.masteryacademy.com | +603 - 2284 8080

DVD Series

Joey Yap's Face Reading Revealed DVD Series

Mian Xiang, the Chinese art of Face Reading, is an ancient form of physiognomy and entails the use of the face and facial characteristics to evaluate key aspects of a person's life, luck and destiny. In his Face Reading DVDs series, Joey Yap shows you how the facial features reveal a wealth of information about a person's luck, destiny and personality.

Mian Xiang also tell us the talents, quirks and personality of an individual. Do you know that just by looking at a person's face, you can ascertain his or her health, wealth, relationships and career? Let Joey Yap show you how the 12 Palaces can be utilised to reveal a person's inner talents, characteristics and much more.

Feng Shui for Homebuyers DVD Series

In these DVDs, you will also learn how to identify properties with good Feng Shui features that will help you promote a fulfilling life and achieve your full potential. Discover how to avoid properties with negative Feng Shui that can bring about detrimental effects to your health, wealth and relationships.

Joey will also elaborate on how to fix the various aspects of your home that may have an impact on the Feng Shui of your property and give pointers on how to tap into the positive energies to support your goals.

Discover Feng Shui with Joey Yap: Set of 4 DVDs
Informative and entertaining, classical Feng Shui comes alive in *Discover Feng Shui with Joey Yap!*

You have the questions. Now let Joey personally answer them in this 4-set DVD compilation! Learn how to ensure the viability of your residence or workplace, Feng Shui-wise, without having to convert it into a Chinese antiques' shop. Classical Feng Shui is about harnessing the natural power of your environment to improve quality of life. It's a systematic and subtle metaphysical science.

Walking the Dragons with Joey Yap (The TV Series)

This DVD set features eight episodes, covering various landform Feng Shui analyses and applications from Joey Yap as he and his co-hosts travel through China. It includes case studies of both modern and historical sites with a focus on Yin House (burial places) Feng Shui and the tombs of the Qing Dynasty emperors.

The series was partly filmed on-location in mainland China, and the state of Selangor, Malaysia.

www.masteryacademy.com | +603 - 2284 8080

Home Study Courses

Gain Valuable Knowledge from the Comfort of Your Home

Now, armed with your trusty computer or laptop and Internet access, knowledge of Chinese Metaphysics is just a click away!

3 easy steps to activate your Home Study Course:

Step 1:
Go to the URL as indicated on the Activation Card, and key in your Activation Code

Step 2:
At the Registration page, fill in the details accordingly to enable us to generate your Student Identification (Student ID).

Step 3:
Upon successful registration, you may begin your lessons immediately.

Joey Yap's Feng Shui Mastery HomeStudy Course

Module 1: **Empowering Your Home**
Module 2: **Master Practitioner Program**

Learn how easy it is to harness the power of the environment to promote health, wealth and prosperity in your life. The knowledge and applications of Feng Shui will no more be a mystery but a valuable tool you can master on your own.

Joey Yap's BaZi Mastery HomeStudy Course

Module 1: **Mapping Your Life**
Module 2: **Mastering Your Future**

Discover your path of least resistance to success with insights about your personality and capabilities, and what strengths you can tap on to maximize your potential for success and happiness by mastering BaZi (Chinese Astrology). This course will teach you all the essentials you need to interpret a BaZi chart and more.

Joey Yap's Mian Xiang Mastery HomeStudy Course

Module 1: **Face Reading**
Module 2: **Advanced Face Reading**

A face can reveal so much about a person. Now, you can learn the art and science of Mian Xiang (Chinese Face Reading) to understand a person's character based on his or her facial features with ease and confidence.

www.masteryacademy.com | +603 - 2284 8080

Feng Shui Mastery™
LIVE COURSES (MODULES ONE TO FOUR)

The Feng Shui Mastery™ comprises Feng Shui Mastery Modules 1, 2, 3 and 4. It starts off with a foundation program up to the advanced practitioner level. It is a thorough, comprehensive program that covers important theories from various classical Feng Shui systems including Ba Zhai, San Yuan, San He, and Xuan Kong.

Module One: Beginners Course

Module Two: Practitioners Course

Module Three: Advanced Practitioners Course

Module Four: Master Course

BaZi Mastery™
LIVE COURSES (MODULES ONE TO FOUR)

The BaZi Mastery™ consists of BaZi Mastery Modules 1, 2, 3 and 4. In Modules 1 and 2, students will receive a thorough introduction to BaZi, along with an intensive understanding of BaZi principles and the requisite skills to practice it with accuracy and precision. This will prepare them, and serious Feng Shui practitioners, for a more advanced levels and fine-tune their application skills in Modules 3 and 4.

Module One: Intensive Foundation Course

Module Two: Practitioners Course

Module Three: Advanced Practitioners Course

Module Four: Master Course in BaZi

XUAN KONG MASTERY™
LIVE COURSES (MODULES ONE TO THREE)
Advanced Courses For Master Practitioners

The Xuan Kong Mastery™ comprises Xuan Kong Mastery Modules 1, 2A, 2B and 3. It is a sophisticated branch of Feng Shui replete with many techniques and formulae, enabling practitioners to evaluate Feng Shui on a more thorough and in-depth basis. The study of Xuan Kong encompasses numerology, symbology and science of the Ba Gua along with the mathematics of time.

Module One: Advanced Foundation Course

Module Two A: Advanced Xuan Kong Methodologies

Module Two B: Purple White

Module Three: Advanced Xuan Kong Da Gua

www.masteryacademy.com | +603 - 2284 8080

Mian Xiang Mastery™
LIVE COURSES (MODULES ONE AND TWO)

The Mian Xiang Mastery™ comprises of Mian Xiang Mastery Modules 1 and 2 to allow students to learn this ancient art in a thorough, detailed manner. Each module has a carefully-developed syllabus that allows students to get acquainted with the fundamentals of Mian Xiang before moving on to the more intricate theories and principles that will enable them to practice Mian Xiang with greater depth and complexity.

Module One:
Basic Face Reading

Module Two:
Practical Face Reading

Yi Jing Mastery™
LIVE COURSES (MODULES ONE AND TWO)

The Yi Jing Mastery™ comprises Modules 1 and 2. Both Modules aim to give casual and serious Yi Jing enthusiasts a serious insight into one of the most important philosophical treatises in ancient Chinese thought. Yi Jing uses sophisticated formulas and calculations to derive the answers to questions we pose. It is a science of divination, and in our classes there is a heavy emphasis on the scientific aspect of it. It bears no religious or superstitious affiliation.

Module One:
Traditional Yi Jing

Module Two:
Plum Blossom Numerology

Ze Ri Mastery™
LIVE COURSES (MODULES ONE AND TWO)

The ZeRi Mastery™ consists of ZeRi Mastery Modules 1 and 2. This program provides students with a thorough introduction to the art of Date Selection both for Personal and Feng Shui purposes. Our ZeRi Mastery™ aims to provide a thorough and comprehensive program on the art of Date Selection, covering everything from Personal and Feng Shui Date Selection to Xuan Kong Da Gua Date Selection.

Module One:
Personal and Feng Shui Date Selection

Module Two:
Xuan Kong Da Gua Date Selection

---

www.masteryacademy.com | +603 - 2284 8080

Feng Shui for Life

This is an entry-level five-day course designed for the Feng Shui beginner to learn the application of practical Feng Shui in day-to-day living. Lessons include quick tips on analyzing the BaZi chart, simple Feng Shui solutions for the home, basic Date Selection, useful Face Reading techniques and practical Water formulas. A great introduction course on Chinese Metaphysics studies for beginners.

Joey Yap's Design Your Destiny

This is a three-day life transformation program designed to inspire awareness and action for you to create a better quality of life. It introduces the DRT™ (Decision Referential Technology) method, which utilizes the BaZi Personality Profiling system to determine the right version of you, and serves as a tool to help you make better decisions and achieve a better life in the least resistant way possible based on your Personality Profile Type.

Walk the Mountains! Learn Feng Shui in a Practical and Hands-on Program

Feng Shui Mastery Excursion™

Learn landform (Luan Tou) Feng Shui by walking the mountains and chasing the Dragon's vein in China. This Program takes the students in a study tour to examine notable Feng Shui landmarks, mountains, hills, valleys, ancient palaces, famous mansions, houses and tombs in China. The Excursion is a 'practical' hands-on course where students are shown to perform readings using the formulas they've learnt and to recognize and read Feng Shui Landform (Luan Tou) formations.

Read about China Excursion here:
http://www.fengshuiexcursion.com

Mastery Academy courses are conducted around the world. Find out when will Joey Yap be in your area by visiting **www.masteryacademy.com** or call our office at **+603-2284 8080**.